For Virgil

A little bit Mr. Bingley,
a little bit Mr. Willoughby, and, of course,
a little bit Mr. Darcy

Jennifer Adams

REMARKABLY JANE

Notable Quotations on Jane Austen

GIBBS SMITH
TO ENRICH AND INSPIRE HUMANKIND
Salt Lake City | Charleston | Santa Fe | Santa Barbara

First Edition
13 12 11 10 09   5 4 3 2 1

Text © 2009 Jennifer Adams

Published by
Gibbs Smith
P.O. Box 667
Layton, Utah 84041

Orders: 1.800.835.4993
www.gibbs-smith.com

Designed by Black Eye Design
Printed and bound in Wisconsin
Gibbs Smith books are printed on either recycled, 100% post-consumer waste, or FSC-certified papers.

Library of Congress Cataloging-in-Publication Data

Remarkably Jane : notable quotations on Jane Austen / Jennifer Adams. — 1st ed.
     p. cm.
  ISBN-13: 978-1-4236-0478-5
  ISBN-10: 1-4236-0478-4
 1. Austen, Jane, 1775-1817—Quotations. 2. Authorship—Quotations, maxims, etc. 3. Quotations, English. I. Adams, Jennifer.
  PR4036.R46 2009
  823'.7—dc22

                              2008037750

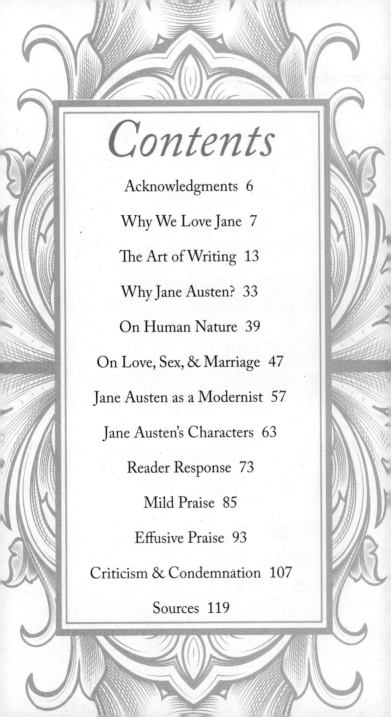

Contents

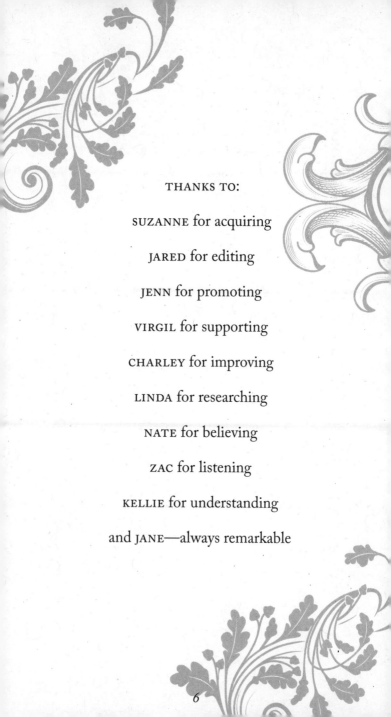

THANKS TO:

SUZANNE for acquiring

JARED for editing

JENN for promoting

VIRGIL for supporting

CHARLEY for improving

LINDA for researching

NATE for believing

ZAC for listening

KELLIE for understanding

and JANE—always remarkable

Why We Love Jane

NOT EVERYONE LOVES JANE AUSTEN. Even among great writers and critics there is a huge divergence of opinion and strong feelings. It's been fascinating and really enjoyable in creating this book to see who likes her and who does not, and what they have to say on the matter.

If you do love her, you know there is nothing as maddening as trying to explain her novels to a friend or coworker who just doesn't get it. On the other hand, there's nothing quite as delightful as presenting her to, say, an attorney in his forties who finds himself converted and tells you that his wife thinks he's gone insane because he goes to the video store for the new James Bond movie and comes home with *Becoming Jane* and *The Jane Austen Book Club* instead.

To those of us who love Jane Austen, she is like the brightness of burnished silver. Something lovely, with sparkle, that makes our world more beautiful. I adore her. I love the pleasure she gives with a well-turned line, the way she can make you actually laugh out loud, the bite of her sarcasm, how she lets you fall in love again and again.

I love that so much of what is real—in life as well as in her books—happens in the rich landscape under the surface of everyday living, in the subtext of our interactions. The layers of meaning behind a glance, saying one thing when the person you're talking to knows it means something else, the electricity of sexual tension between two people that is contained and unacknowledged. We may no longer go to balls or wear shoe-roses or eat petit fours, but we can still sit with someone at lunch, eating a salad and talking about nothing, and what we're really thinking is how beautiful they are and how we want to reach up and touch their face.

In our lives, as in Austen's world, there are limits imposed on us by the family into which we are born, real pain still comes from a cruel remark in a social setting, people we thought we loved deceive us in profound ways, we still try to make sense of who we are in a complicated world of survival. And we all still look for happiness.

People who don't like Jane Austen often complain that in her novels "nothing happens." It is true that in her books there are no government conspiracies, no kidnappings, no fast-paced action scenes. What does happen happens in the mind and in the heart. What happens is all about love and sex and money and marriage and power and position, and perhaps, most importantly, the emergence of the individual through all of these entanglements, who learns how to define and maintain her own identity and also somehow—remarkably and yet believably—finds happiness. *Everything* happens in Jane Austen. At least everything that matters.

—JENNIFER ADAMS

"I must make use of this opportunity to thank you . . . for the very high praise you bestow on my . . . novels. I am too vain to wish to convince you that you have praised them beyond their merit."

—JANE AUSTEN

The Art of Writing

I never wanted to be famous, and I never dreamt I would be famous. . . . I IMAGINED BEING A FAMOUS WRITER would be like being like Jane Austen. Being able to sit at home in the parsonage and your books would be very famous and occasionally you would correspond with the Prince of Wales's secretary."

—J. K. ROWLING, 2003
AUTHOR OF THE HARRY POTTER SERIES

"I am inclined to say in desperation, read it yourself and KICK OUT EVERY SENTENCE THAT ISN'T AS JANE AUSTEN WOULD HAVE WRITTEN IT IN PROSE. Which is, I admit, impossible. But when you *do* get a limpid line in perfectly straight normal order, isn't it worth any other ten?"

—EZRA POUND, 1938
POET

"I DO THINK NOVELS ARE EXTREMELY
IMPORTANT. And, like Jane Austen,
I don't think their importance is measured
by the amount of fizzing and popping
and width of stage."

—IAN MCEWAN, 2002
NOVELIST

I love structure

in the novel. It's not surprising that overwhelmingly my favorite novelist is Jane Austen—structure is tremendously important to her. I LOVE THE IDEA OF BRINGING ORDER OUT OF DISORDER, WHICH IS WHAT THE MYSTERY IS ABOUT."

—P. D. JAMES, 1998
MYSTERY NOVELIST

"Nothing very much happens in her books and yet, when you come to the bottom of a page, you eagerly turn it to learn what will happen next. Nothing very much does and again you eagerly turn the page. THE NOVELIST WHO HAS THE POWER TO ACHIEVE THIS HAS THE MOST PRECIOUS GIFT A NOVELIST CAN POSSESS."

—W. SOMERSET MAUGHAM, 1955
PLAYWRIGHT AND NOVELIST

Has any writer

ever painted a truer picture of the thoughts,

perceptions, motives (conscious and

unconscious), speech, and behavior of men

and women in everyday life, or one more

entertaining, or more subtly shaded, or

finely drawn, than we find on every page

in the novels of Jane Austen?"

—PATRICE HANNON, 2007
AUTHOR OF *Dear Jane Austen: A Heroine's Guide to Life and Love*

"JANE AUSTEN IS WEIRDLY CAPABLE OF KEEPING EVERYBODY BUSY.

The moralists, the Eros-and-Agape people, the Marxists, the Freudians, the Jungians, the semioticians, the deconstructors—all find an adventurous playground in six samey novels about middle-class provincials. And for every generation of critics, and readers, HER FICTION EFFORTLESSLY RENEWS ITSELF."

—MARTIN AMIS, 1996
NOVELIST, ESSAYIST,
AND SHORT STORY WRITER

"[Jane Austen's novels] appear to be compact of abject truth. Their events are excruciatingly unimportant; and yet ... they will probably outlast all Fielding, Scott, George Eliot, Thackery, and Dickens. THE ART IS SO CONSUMMATE THAT THE SECRET IS HIDDEN; peer at them as hard as one may; shake them; take them apart; one cannot see how it is done."

—THORNTON WILDER, 1938
PLAYWRIGHT AND NOVELIST,
WINNER OF THE PULITZER PRIZE

Every writer

stands on the shoulders of the old authors who have shaped and refined language and storytelling. In my mind, almost no one today approaches their greatness in either style or insight. I think I have read *Pride and Prejudice*—in my view the most perfect book in our language—eight times, and it has taught me something new each time."

—LAURA HILLENBRAND, 2001
AUTHOR OF *Seabiscuit*

"Also read again and for the third time at least Miss Austen's very finely written novel of *Pride and Prejudice*. THAT YOUNG LADY HAD A TALENT FOR DESCRIBING THE INVOLVEMENT AND FEELINGS AND CHARACTERS of ordinary life which is to me the most wonderful I ever met with. The Big Bow-wow strain I can do myself like any now going, but the exquisite touch which renders ordinary commonplace things and characters interesting from the truth of the description and the sentiment is denied to me. What a pity such a gifted creature died so early!"

—SIR WALTER SCOTT, 1826
HISTORICAL NOVELIST AND POET

"When people COMPARE SHAKESPEARE WITH JANE AUSTEN, they may mean that the minds of both had consumed all impediments; and for that reason we do not know Jane Austen and we do not know Shakespeare, and for that reason Jane Austen pervades every word she wrote, and so does Shakespeare."

—VIRGINIA WOOLF, 1913
ESSAYIST AND NOVELIST

Yes, she was witty and clever and structurally brilliant, but I think most of all she was honest and wrote completely from the heart."

—JOE WRIGHT, 2005
DIRECTOR OF THE 2005 FILM VERSION OF
Pride and Prejudice

I love fiction

and I love traditional fiction writing, but I don't believe that every book has to be something written by Jane Austen out of the nineteenth century. I don't believe that there's just one way to write a novel."

—MICHAEL ONDAATJE, 2007
NOVELIST

"The best books, by and large, are written by people who don't do a great deal of research, who don't follow my pattern. WHO JUST SIT DOWN IN A LITTLE ROOM LIKE THIS WITH A TYPEWRITER AND MAYBE A WORD PROCESSOR, SOME MAPS, AND WRITE A GREAT BOOK. . . . That's what Jane Austen did."

—JAMES MICHENER, 1971
NOVELIST, WINNER OF THE PULITZER PRIZE

"There have been several revolutions of taste during the last century and a quarter of English literature, and through them all PERHAPS ONLY TWO REPUTATIONS HAVE NEVER BEEN AFFECTED BY THE SHIFTS OF FASHION: Shakespeare's and Jane Austen's."

—EDMUND WILSON, 1944
LITERARY CRITIC

I think

that every woman writer who has written about family life gets compared to Jane Austen. IT IS A LAZY COMPARISON, HOWEVER FLATTERING."

—ANITA DESAI, 2007
NOVELIST

The plot of *Bridget Jones* was actually stolen from *Pride and Prejudice*. I thought that Jane Austen's plots were very good and have been market researched over a number of centuries, so I would simply steal it. 'Cause I thought she wouldn't mind and anyway she's dead."

—HELEN FIELDING, 2001
AUTHOR OF *Bridget Jones's Diary*

"MANY GREAT NOVELS HAVE BEEN WRITTEN ABOUT THE EVERYDAY —Jane Austen and so on. But you need a SUPERB ART to make that sort of thing interesting."

—GORE VIDAL, 1974
NOVELIST, SCREENWRITER, AND ESSAYIST

"There are some writers who wrote too much. There are others who wrote enough. THERE ARE YET OTHERS WHO WROTE NOTHING LIKE ENOUGH TO SATISFY THEIR ADMIRERS, and Jane Austen is certainly one of these."

—MARGARET DRABBLE, 1974
NOVELIST

Why
Jane Austen?

What is all this about Jane Austen? What is there *in* her? What is it all about?"

—JOSEPH CONRAD, 1901
NOVELIST

"How did this early-nineteenth-century novelist become THE CHICK-LIT, CHICK-FLICK QUEEN FOR TODAY? It is not only because she is an enduring writer. So is Melville, but bumper stickers and T-shirts read "What would Jane do?" not "What would Herman do?"

—CARYN JAMES, 2007
FILM CRITIC FOR *The New York Times*

"The key to Jane Austen's fortune
with posterity has been in part the

EXTRAORDINARY GRACE OF HER FACILITY . . .

little master-strokes of imagination."

—HENRY JAMES, 1905
NOVELIST

She speaks

to women in a way that perhaps men
will never understand fully, which I think
is rather wonderful."

—PAUL JACOBS, 2005
PRODUCER OF THE 2005 FILM VERSION OF
Pride and Prejudice

On Human Nature

You could not

shock her more than she shocks me;

Beside her Joyce seems innocent as grass.

It makes me most uncomfortable to see

An English spinster of the middle class

Describe the amorous effects of 'brass,'

Reveal so frankly and with such sobriety

The economic base of society."

—W. H. AUDEN, 1937
POET

"Austen tells us HOW MUCH WE HAVE TO SUFFER IN ORDER TO FIND REAL LOVE and truth as well as the pain of growing up. These conflicts in one way or another determine our lives."

—ANG LEE, 1995
DIRECTOR OF THE 1995 FILM VERSION OF
Sense and Sensibility

"I'm most interested in human behavior, which is probably why I'M SUCH A PUSHOVER for Jane Austen."

—EMMA THOMPSON, 2006
SCREENWRITER AND ACTRESS PORTRAYING ELINOR
IN THE 1995 FILM VERSION OF *Sense and Sensibility*

"TO UNDERSTAND THE HUMAN CONDITION YOU HAVE TO HAVE BEEN PAINED BY THE HUMAN EXPERIENCE. . . . Nearly immediately after [she was separated from Tom LeFroy] she started writing *Pride and Prejudice*, she had this huge flurry of activity that showed a great understanding of the human condition, not just love stories, but, really what it is to be alive."

—JAMES MCAVOY, 2008
ACTOR PORTRAYING TOM LEFROY IN
Becoming Jane

F or those of us who suspect all the mysteries of life are contained in the microcosm of the family, THAT PERSONAL RELATIONSHIPS PREFIGURE ALL ELSE, the work of Jane Austen is the Rosetta stone of literature."

—ANNA QUINDLEN, 1995
NOVELIST

Why shouldn't

a work of fantasy be as truthful and
profound about becoming an adult human
being as the work of
George Eliot or Jane Austen?"

—PHILIP PULLMAN, 1998
AUTHOR OF *His Dark Materials* SERIES

If charity

is the poetry of conduct and honour
the rhetoric of conduct, Jane Austen's
'principles' might be described as the
grammar of conduct."

—C. S. LEWIS, 1954
AUTHOR OF *The Chronicles of Narnia*

On Love, Sex, & Marriage

"Affection [is] a word that Austen values over *love. Affection* between a woman and man, in Austen,

IS THE MORE PROFOUND AND

LASTING EMOTION."

—*HAROLD BLOOM,* 1994
LITERARY CRITIC

Look through

the lattice-work of her neat sentences, joined together with bright nails of craftsmanship, painted with the gay varnish of wit, and you will see women haggard with desire or triumphant with love, whose delicate reactions to men make the heroines of all our later novels seem merely to turn signs, 'Stop' or 'Go' toward the advancing male."

—REBECCA WEST, 1928
NOVELIST AND JOURNALIST

"I also think . . . that the reason no one married [Jane Austen] was the same reason Crosby didn't publish *Northanger Abbey*. IT WAS ALL JUST TOO MUCH. Something truly frightening rumbled there beneath the bubbling mirth: something capable of taking the world by its heels, and shaking it."

—FAY WELDON, 1984
NOVELIST

I'm just as interested in the love story between the sisters [in *Sense and Sensibility*] as I am in seeing Marianne [and Elinor fall in love]. . . . It's as much about family as it is about love."

—EMMA THOMPSON, 1995
SCREENWRITER AND ACTRESS PORTRAYING ELINOR
IN THE 1995 FILM VERSION OF *Sense and Sensibility*

Was Jane Austen gay? This question, posed by the normally staid *London Review of Books,* was the headline for an essay by Stanford professor Terry Castle that subtly explored the 'unconscious homoerotic dimension' of Austen's letters to her sister Cassandra. The implication caused quite a kerfuffle among Austenites."

—BELINDA LUSCOMBE, 1995
WRITER FOR *Time* MAGAZINE

"One of Jane Austen's greatest talents
is that she presents sexual tension with
such subtlety."

—JOAN KLINGEL RAY, 2005
PRESIDENT OF THE JANE AUSTEN SOCIETY
OF NORTH AMERICA, 2000–2006

"For all the body's powers and vulnerability,
[Austen's] novels demonstrate that, for her,
the real dance of life lies in language and in
understanding."

—CAROL SHIELDS, 2001
BIOGRAPHER OF JANE AUSTEN, WINNER OF
THE PULITZER PRIZE

"EVERYONE THINKS SHE'S ELIZABETH BENNET; NOT EVERYONE THINKS SHE'S JANE EYRE. Everyone knows a young woman trying to decide if the guy she's attracted to is Mr. Right. Not everyone meets a Mr. Right who has a mad wife in the attic."

—MARSHA HUFF, 2007
PRESIDENT OF THE JANE AUSTEN SOCIETY OF
NORTH AMERICA, 2007–PRESENT

Nudity, sexual abuse, lesbianism, a dash of incest—will we never tire of Jane Austen?"

—ANTHONY LANE, 1999
FILM REVIEWER FOR *The New Yorker*

Jane Austen as a Modernist

Her work is not just social comedy. It's about MONEY, STRUGGLE FOR INDIVIDUALISM, SEX—all the kinds of things that interest us now. People sometimes misinterpret that. Jane Austen is regarded as such a prim writer. Well, she's not, really. The engine of her plot is often sexual desire."

—ANDREW DAVIES, 2008
SCREENWRITER OF THE 1995 BBC TV MINISERIES
Pride and Prejudice

"IN AUSTEN'S NOVELS, THERE ARE SPACES FOR OPPOSITIONS that do not need to eliminate each other in order to exist. There is also space—not just space but a necessity—for self-reflection and self-criticism."

—AZAR NAFISI, 2004
AUTHOR OF *Reading Lolita in Tehran*

"[Jane Austen's world] is an art which simultaneously acknowledges an abroad, an empire, outside of the site of the text, and declines to have much to do with it. INSTEAD IT DIRECTS ITS FOCUS, AND THE READER'S ENERGIES, UPON THE CREATION OF AN INTERIOR LIFE OF THE SELF, that interior life which is not the birthright but the prize of modernity. Austen's England is then, in effect, the contemporary world."

—JOHN WILTSHIRE, 2006
JANE AUSTEN SCHOLAR

When you begin to love Austen, her world doesn't seem that antiquated. Her characters worry about money, deal with embarrassing family members, cringe at social slights, and spend more time than they should hoping to fall in love, even when the local prospects don't seem that promising."

—ROBIN SWICORD, 2007
DIRECTOR OF THE FILM VERSION OF
The Jane Austen Book Club

Jane Austen's
Characters

It is impossible

not to feel in every line of *Pride and Prejudice,* in every word of Elizabeth, the entire want of taste which could produce so pert, so worldly a heroine as the beloved of such a man as Darcy. Wickham is equally bad. Oh! They were just fit for each other, and I cannot forgive that delightful Darcy for parting them."

—MARY RUSSELL MITFORD, 1814
NOVELIST AND PLAYWRIGHT

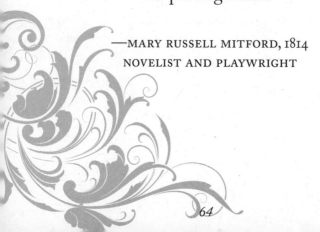

Emma, the heroine, is treated almost mercilessly. In every passage of the book she is at fault for some folly, some vanity, some ignorance, —or indeed for some meanness. . . . Nowadays we dare not make our heroines so little."

—ANTHONY TROLLOPE, 1870
NOVELIST

"[Mr. Darcy] may appear to be aloof, arrogant, haughty, pompous, prideful, but he's just misunderstood. HE'S SHY, I THINK, IS WHAT IT IS. He's just shy."

—MATTHEW MACFADYEN, 2005
ACTOR PORTRAYING MR. DARCY IN THE 2005 FILM
VERSION OF *Pride and Prejudice*

"EDMUND AND FANNY ARE BOTH MORALLY DETESTABLE and the endorsement of their feelings and behaviour by the author ... makes *Mansfield Park* an immoral book."

—KINGSLEY AMIS, 1957
NOVELIST AND POET

It wasn't really me that everyone went crazy about—it was the character [Fitzwilliam Darcy], who'd been around for a couple of centuries."

—COLIN FIRTH, 1997
ACTOR PORTRAYING MR. DARCY IN THE
1995 BBC TV MINISERIES *Pride and Prejudice*

"With *Sense and Sensibility,* you can't help feeling that the GUYS WHO GET THE GIRLS just aren't good enough."

—ANDREW DAVIES, 2007
SCREENWRITER OF THE 2008 *Masterpiece Theatre*
VERSION OF *Sense and Sensibility*

"Elizabeth [Bennet] has a thousand faults . . . IS OFTEN BLIND, PERT, AUDACIOUS, IMPRUDENT; and yet how splendidly she comes out of it all! Alive to the very tips of her fingers."

—UNSIGNED ARTICLE IN *The Academy,* 1898

Anne Elliot,

though subdued, is the creation for whom Austen herself must have felt the most affection, because she lavished her own gifts upon Anne."

—HAROLD BLOOM, 1994
LITERARY CRITIC

"A writer must rub his characters with generosity and humor for them to be bearable at all. This is their salt and black pepper. Jane Austen additionally SETS THEM IN THE HEAVY CROCKERY AND ROASTS THEM ALL NIGHT WITH LEMONS AND HORSERADISH, and the bitterness merely improves the overall joy."

—LEIF ENGER, 2008
AUTHOR OF *Peace Like a River*

*R*eader
*R*esponse

Each of us has a private Austen.

—KAREN JOY FOWLER, 2004
AUTHOR OF *The Jane Austen Book Club*

"There would be more genuine rejoicing at the discovery OF A COMPLETE NEW NOVEL BY JANE AUSTEN than any other literary discovery, short of a new major play by Shakespeare."

—MARGARET DRABBLE, 1974
NOVELIST

Jane Austen?

I feel that I am approaching dangerous ground. The reputation of Jane Austen is surrounded by cohorts of defenders who are ready to do murder for their sacred cause."

—ARNOLD BENNETT, 1927
LITERARY CRITIC

"My two heroes: Jane Austen and Tolstoy."

—JOHN GARDNER, 1981
NOVELIST AND TEACHER

"As to the critics hostile to Jane Austen, from Victorian times onwards, THEY HAVE BEEN EITHER TEMPERAMENTALLY OFF KEY like Charlotte Brontë, Mark Twain, or [D. H.] Lawrence, or insufficiently informed."

—ANGUS WILSON, 1968
NOVELIST AND SHORT STORY WRITER

"I like to read NOVELS OF PSYCHOLOGICAL SUSPENSE .... I like Jane Austen, Henry James, Joyce Porter."

—MARTHA GRIMES, 2001
MYSTERY NOVELIST

"Everybody believes in some way that THEY ARE LIZZIE BENNET."

—KEIRA KNIGHTLEY, 2005
ACTRESS PORTRAYING ELIZABETH BENNET IN THE
2005 FILM VERSION OF *Pride and Prejudice*

The critics of the day were in the dark. [Jane Austen] was not conscious herself of founding a new school of fiction, which would inspire new canons of criticism."

—UNSIGNED REVIEW IN *The Academy*, 1870

I think, the fact that we have fallen in love with Elizabeth Bennet ... means, in effect, that we have fallen in love with Jane Austen; and once we do that we are her lovers for life."

—FRANK SWINNERTON, 1940
LITERARY CRITIC AND NOVELIST

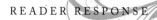
I've never read

a Jane Austen novel in my life."

—STEPHEN KING, 1997
NOVELIST AND SHORT STORY WRITER

"I've been talked about in the same context
as Jane Austen. I DIDN'T STICK THAT LABEL
ON MYSELF, OTHER PEOPLE DID. Quite
inaccurate. I've never got on very well with
Jane Austen."

—ANITA BROOKNER, 2001
NOVELIST

"I think the next writer to have a really big influence on me was Jane Austen. *Pride and Prejudice* was one of the books that I read backwards and forwards. I REALLY WANTED TO BE ELIZABETH BENNET. Of course, today, there are people who would say, 'Oh, that's so Anglo'; they think I should have been more influenced by Chinese opera or something."

—GISH JEN, 1993
NOVELIST

I'd rather be reading Jane Austen.

—BUMPER STICKER

Mild Praise

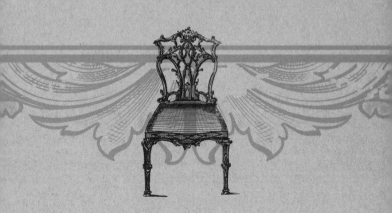

"I was a little mortified to find you had not admitted the name of Miss Austen into your list of favorites. . . . SHE IS PLEASING, INTERESTING, EQUABLE, YET AMUSING. I count on your making some apology for this omission."

—CHIEF JUSTICE JOHN MARSHALL, 1826
AMERICAN STATESMAN AND CHIEF JUSTICE
OF THE SUPREME COURT

Miss Austen

has never been so popular

as she deserved to be."

—THOMAS HENRY LISTER, 1830
NOVELIST

"Since I was twelve or so, I'VE LOVED NINETEENTH-CENTURY NOVELS. I'm a complete sucker for those. I still read them. Every few years when I've forgotten enough Jane Austen I read them all again."

—ANN BRASHARES, 2001
AUTHOR OF *The Sisterhood of the Traveling Pants*

You know

I love middle-class tragedies and the
little squabbles that build up family life in
England. I have had delightful letters from
you quite in the style of Jane Austen."

—OSCAR WILDE, 1897
PLAYWRIGHT

"For some years I've been going around saying, 'Look, what is this comparison [of my work] with Jane Austen? I never got on with her at university, and I haven't even read all her novels.' AS A YOUNG MAN OF TWENTY-TWO OR TWENTY-THREE, SHE WAS TOO GIRLY FOR ME. I hadn't developed a sufficiently mature sensibility to appreciate that she's a really great writer. . . . I've since become her greatest fan."

—KAZUO ISHIGURO, 2005
NOVELIST

M_y
favorite-favorite
is probably Jane Austen."

—STEPHENIE MEYER, 2007
AUTHOR OF THE *Twilight* SERIES

Effusive Praise

Jane lies

in Winchester—blessed be her shade!

Praise the Lord for making her,
and her for all she made!

And while the stones of Winchester,
or Milsom Street, remain,

Glory, love, and honor
unto England's Jane."

—RUDYARD KIPLING, 1924
POET, WINNER OF THE NOBEL PRIZE

"THE WIT OF JANE AUSTEN
has for partner
the perfection of her taste."

—VIRGINIA WOOLF, 1925
ESSAYIST AND NOVELIST

"Jane Austen, of course, WISE IN HER
NEATNESS, TRIM IN HER SEDATENESS;
she never fails, but there are few or none
like her."

—EDITH WHARTON, 1925
NOVELIST, WINNER OF THE PULITZER PRIZE

We love her because
we love her thoughts, her words,
her delicious way of looking askance at the
world. . . . Who else in all of history would
we rather sit beside at a boring meeting
than the woman who once said, 'I do not
want people to be very agreeable, as
it saves me the trouble of liking them a
great deal.'"

—SHANNON HALE, 2007
AUTHOR OF *Austenland*

"Miss Austen has always been
par excellence
the favourite author of literary men."

—UNSIGNED REVIEW IN *The Academy*, 1870

"Jane Austen is in fact one of the most
lasting of English novelists. She 'wears
well,' as they say in England. Make
friends with this quiet but brilliant woman,
this superb artist in fiction, and you have
made a friend for life."

—J. B. PRIESTLEY, 1960
NOVELIST AND PLAYWRIGHT

"I am a Jane Austenite, and therefore slightly imbecile about Jane Austen. She is my favourite author! I READ AND RE-READ, THE MOUTH OPEN AND THE MIND CLOSED. . . . The Jane Austenite possesses little of the brightness he ascribes so freely to his idol. Like all regular churchgoers, he scarcely notices what is being said."

—E. M. FORSTER, 1924
NOVELIST

"By page 60 [of *Pride and Prejudice*],
I found myself CRYING INTO MY PINT
OF LAGER, and laughing out loud at parts.
I thought it was the most consuming
piece of character observation. You can't
not be a fan, really."

—JOE WRIGHT, 2005
DIRECTOR OF THE 2005 FILM VERSION OF
Pride and Prejudice

"THE GAIETY IS UNEXTINGUISHED, the irony has kept its bite, the reasoning is still sweet, the sparkle undiminished.... Jane Austen's work [is] irresistible and as nearly flawless as any fiction could be."

—EUDORA WELTY, 1969
NOVELIST, WINNER OF THE PULITZER PRIZE

"THERE MAY NOT BE A NOVELIST, in English, who surpasses Jane Austen."

—HAROLD BLOOM, 2000
LITERARY CRITIC

Jane Austen

was born before those bonds which (we are told) protected women from truth, were burst by the Brontës or elaborately untied by George Eliot. YET THE FACT REMAINS THAT JANE AUSTEN KNEW MORE ABOUT MEN THAN EITHER OF THEM. Jane Austen may have been protected from truth; but it was precious little truth that was protected from her."

—G. K. CHESTERTON, 1913
LITERARY CRITIC, PLAYWRIGHT, AND NOVELIST

"Jane Austen still bewitches me.

I KNOW HOW IT'S ALL GOING TO COME OUT

but she still delights me."

— MARY STOLZ, 1975
YOUNG ADULT NOVELIST

I worship
Jane Austen.

—ANNE TYLER, 2006
NOVELIST, WINNER OF THE PULITZER PRIZE

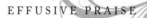

All I want to be is the Jane Austen of south Alabama."

—HARPER LEE, 1964
NOVELIST, WINNER OF THE PULITZER PRIZE

No burden weighs more heavily on a writer's shoulders than that of being MUCH LOVED, but something unreachable in Austen shrugs off the weight."

—ANTHONY LANE, 1996
FILM REVIEWER FOR *The New Yorker*

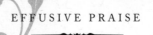

That Jane!

For a quiet spinster who rarely ventured farther than Bath, she does get around."

—PATRICIA T. O'CONNER, 2004
WRITER FOR *The New York Times*

"LONG AFTER THE LITERARY PENDANTS

HAVE NUMBERED EVERY COBBLESTONE IN

ENGLAND, Jane Austen's novels will still be

. . . soothing the souls of ordinary cultivated

readers."

—MICHAEL A. SCULLY, 1983
LITERARY CRITIC

J ane Austen ... got as close to perfection as anyone can."

—SUSANNA CLARKE, 2004
AUTHOR OF *Jonathan Strange & Mr. Norrell*

Criticism & Condemnation

Every time

I read *Pride and Prejudice* I want to dig
her up and hit her over the skull with her
own shin-bone."

—MARK TWAIN, 1898
NOVELIST

"[Austen was] a rather heartless little cynic ... PENNING SATIRES ABOUT HER NEIGHBORS WHILST THE DYNASTS WERE TEARING THE WORLD TO PIECES and consigning millions to their graves.... Not a breath from the whirlwind around her ever touched her Chippendale chiffonier or escritoire."

—FREDERIC HARRISON, 1917
BRITISH JURIST AND HISTORIAN

"THIS OLD MAID TYPIFIES 'PERSONALITY' INSTEAD OF CHARACTER, the sharp knowing in apartness instead of knowing in togetherness, and she is, to my feeling, thoroughly unpleasant, English in the bad, mean, snobbish sense of the word."

—D. H. LAWRENCE, 1931
NOVELIST, ESSAYIST, AND POET

"I HAVE NEVER READ ANYTHING Austen wrote. I just never got at reading *Pride and Prejudice* or *Sense and Sensibility*. They seemed to be the Bobbsey Twins for grown-ups."

—ANDY ROONEY, 1999
HUMORIST

I am at a loss

to understand why people hold Miss

Austen's novels at so high a rate, which

seems to me . . . WITHOUT GENIUS, WIT, OR

KNOWLEDGE OF THE WORLD. Never was life

so pinched and narrow."

—RALPH WALDO EMERSON, 1861
ESSAYIST AND POET

"What a strange lecture comes next in your letter! You say I must familiarize my mind with the fact that 'Miss Austen is not a poetess, has no "sentiment"' (you scornfully enclose the word in inverted commas), 'no eloquence, none of the ravishing enthusiasm of poetry'; and then you add, I must 'learn to acknowledge her as one of the greatest artists, one of the greatest painters of human character, and one of the writers with the nicest sense of means to an end that ever lived.' The last point only will I ever acknowledge. Can there be a great artist without poetry?"

—CHARLOTTE BRONTË, 1848
NOVELIST

The function of the British army in the novels of Jane Austen is to look cute at parties."

—SALMON RUSHDIE, 2005
NOVELIST, POLITICAL FIGURE

No female novelist could be less like Jane Austen than Colette, but they share an unfortunate distinction: it is difficult to love either without finding oneself enrolled in a club."

—GABRIELE ANNAN, 1984
LITERARY CRITIC FOR
The New York Review of Books

"How often need we be hit by that first line from *Pride and Prejudice?* Must we continue to suffer from the likes of:

'IT IS A TRUTH UNIVERSALLY ACKNOWLEDGED THAT A CORNED-BEEF SANDWICH ON RYE WILL BE IN WANT OF A PICKLE!'

(displayed in a Delicatessen window)."

—JULIA BRAUN KESSLER, 2007
EDITOR AND JOURNALIST

R eally it is time
this comic patronage of
Jane Austen ceased."

—REBECCA WEST, 1928
NOVELIST AND JOURNALIST

In order to

enjoy her books without disturbance,

those who retain the conventional notion

of her work must always have had slightly

to misread what she wrote."

—D. W. HARDING, 1940
LITERARY CRITIC

Sources

epigraph. Jane Austen, quoted in *Jane Austen: 'My Dear Cassandra'* (London: Collins & Brown, 1990).

page 14. J. K. Rowling, quoted at www.bloomsbury.com.

page 15. Ezra Pound, *Letters from Ezra Pound,* ed. D. D. Paige (New York: Harcourt, Brace, and World, 1950), 308.

page 16. Ian McEwan, quoted at http://books.guardian.co.uk.

page 17. P. D. James, quoted at www.salon.com.

page 18. W. Somerset Maugham, quoted at www.joemckeever .com.

page 19. Patrice Hannon, *Dear Jane Austen: A Heroine's Guide to Life and Love* (New York: Plume, 2007), xiii.

page 20. Martin Amis, "Jane's World," *New Yorker,* January 8, 1996, 34.

page 21. Thornton Wilder, "A Preface for *Our Town*" (1938), in *American Characteristics and Other Essays* (New York: Harper & Row, 1979), 101.

page 22. Laura Hillenbrand, quoted at www.randomhouse.com.

page 23. Sir Walter Scott, quoted in *Jane Austen: 'My Dear Cassandra'* (London: Collins & Brown, 1990), 110.

page 24. Virginia Woolf, *A Room of One's Own* (New York: Harcourt, Brace, Jovanovich, 1957), 50–51.

page 25. Joe Wright, *Pride and Prejudice* 2005 movie, special features.

page 26. Michael Ondaatje, quoted at http://fullmoonfever .wordpress.com.

page 27. James Michener, quoted at www.achievement.org.

page 28. Edmund Wilson, "A Long Talk about Jane Austen," *New Yorker,* June 24, 1944, 69.

page 29. Anita Desai, quoted at www.randomhouse.com.

page 30. Helen Fielding, interview, *Bridget Jones's Diary* movie, special features.

page 31. Gore Vidal, "The Art of Fiction," *Paris Review* 59.

page 31. Margaret Drabble, "Introduction," *Lady Susan; The Watsons; Sandition* (Harmondworth, England: Penguin, 1974), 7.

page 34. John Wiltshire, quoted in B. C. Southam, ed., *Critical Essays on Jane Austen* (London: Routledge & Kegan Paul, 1968), xiii.

page 35. Caryn James, "Austen Powers: Making Jane Sexy," *The New York Times,* July 29, 2007.

page 36. Henry James, "The Lesson of Balzac," in Leon Edel, ed., *The House of Fiction* (London: Rupert Hart-Davis, 1957), 63.

page 37. Paul Jacobs, *Pride and Prejudice* 2005 movie, special features.

page 40. W. H. Auden and Louis MacNeice, *Letters from Iceland* (New York: Random House, 1937), 21.

page 41. Ang Lee, quoted at http://members.tripod.com /~warlight/AUSTEN.html.

page 41. Terry Lawson, © Detroit Free Press, 2006, quoted at www.popmatters.com.

page 42. James McAvoy, quoted at www.britfilms.tv, © 2008 BritFilms TV Limited.

page 43. Anna Quindlen, "Introduction," *Pride and Prejudice* (New York: Modern Library Edition, 2000), viii.

page 44. Philip Pullman, quoted at www.hisdarkmaterials.org.

page 45. C. S. Lewis, "A Note on Jane Austen," in Ian Watt, ed., *Jane Austen: A Collection of Critical Essays* (Englewood Cliffs, New Jersey: Prentice-Hall, 1963), 33.

page 48. Harold Bloom, *The Western Canon* (New York: Riverhead Books, 1994), 237.

page 49. Rebecca West, *The Strange Necessity* (London: Jonathan Cape, 1928), 264.

page 50. Fay Weldon, *Letters to Alice on First Reading Jane Austen* (New York: Taplinger, 1985), 97.

SOURCES

page 51. Bruce Kirkland, "Making Sense of Austen's Classic," *Toronto Sun*, December 7, 1995.

page 52. Belinda Luscombe, "Which Persuasion?" *Time*, August 14, 1995, 73.

page 53. Alessandra Stanley, "Oh, Mr. Darcy . . . Yes, I Said Yes!" *New York Times*, November 20, 2005.

page 53. Carol Shields, *Jane Austen: A Life* (New York: Penguin, 2001), 182.

page 54. Marsha Huff, quoted in "Austen Powers: Making Jane Sexy," *The New York Times*, July 29, 2007.

page 55. Anthony Lane, "All over the Map," *New Yorker*, November 29, 1999, 140.

page 58. Andrew Davies, quoted at www.princegeorge citizen.com.

page 59. Azar Nafisi, *Reading Lolita in Tehran* (New York: Random House, 2004), 268.

page 60. John Wiltshire, *Jane Austen Introductions and Interviews* (New York: Palgrave Macmillan, 2006), 120.

page 61. Robin Swicord, quoted at http://janeaustensworld .wordpress.com.

page 64. Mary Russell Mitford, *Life of Mary Russell Mitford*, ed. A. G. L'Estrange (New York: Harper & Brothers, 1870), 1:300.

page 65. Anthony Trollope, "Miss Austen's Timidity," in David Lodge, ed., *Jane Austen's Emma: A Casebook* (Houndsmill, Basingstoke, Hampshire, and London: Macmillan Education, 1991), 51.

page 66. Matthew MacFadyen, *Pride and Prejudice Diaries*, Part 4.

page 67. Kingsley Amis, "What Became of Jane Austen?" in Ian Watt, ed., *Jane Austen: A Collection of Critical Essays* (Englewood Cliffs, New Jersey: Prentice-Hall, 1963), 142.

page 68. Colin Firth interview, *Radio Times*, July 12, 1997.

page 69. Andrew Davies, quoted at www.walesonline.co.uk.

page 69. *The Academy* 53 (January/June 1898): 262.

page 70. Harold Bloom, *The Western Canon* (New York: Riverhead Books, 1994), 237–38.

page 71. Leif Enger, personal correspondence with the author, 2008.

page 74. Karen Joy Fowler, *The Jane Austen Book Club* (New York: G. P. Putnam's Sons, 2004), 1.

page 75. Margaret Drabble, "Introduction," *Lady Susan; The Watsons; Sandition* (Harmondsworth, England: Penguin, 1974), 7.

page 76. Arnold Bennett, *The Author's Craft and Other Critical Writings of Arnold Bennett*, ed. Samuel Hynes (Lincoln: University of Nebraska Press, 1968), 256.

page 77. John Gardner, radio interview, quoted at http://wired forbooks.org/johngardner.

page 77. Angus Wilson, "The Neighbourhood of Tombuctoo: Conflicts in Jane Austen's Novels," in B. C. Southam, ed., *Critical Essays on Jane Austen* (London: Routledge & Kegan Paul, 1968), 186.

page 78. Martha Grimes, quoted at www.bookreporter.com.

page 78. Keira Knightley, *Pride and Prejudice Diaries*, Part 1.

page 79. *The Academy* 1 (February 12, 1870): 118.

page 80. Frank Swinnerton in "Publisher's Preface," *Pride and Prejudice: The 100 Greatest Books Ever Written* (Norwalk, Connecticut: The Easton Press, 1996), v.

page 81. Stephen King, *60 Minutes* interview, February 16, 1997.

page 81. Anita Brookner, quoted at http://books.guardian.co.uk.

page 82. Y. Matsukawa, "Melus Interview: Gish Jen," *Melus* 18, no. 4 (Winter 1993): 111.

page 86. A. J. Beveridge, *Life of John Marshall* (Boston: Houghton Mifflin, 1916–1919), 4:79–80.

page 87. [Thomas Henry Lister], unsigned review of Catherine Gore, *Women As They Are*, in *Edinburgh Review*, July 1830, 448.

page 88. Ann Brashares, quoted at www.powells.com.

SOURCES

page 89. Oscar Wilde, *The Complete Letters of Oscar Wilde* (London: Fourth Estate, 2000).

page 90. Kazuo Ishiguro, quoted at www.theatlantic.com.

page 91. Stephenie Meyer, "Stephenie Meyer's 'Twilight' Zone," *Entertainment Weekly*, www.ew.com.

page 94. Rudyard Kipling, "The Janeites," in Craig Raine, ed., *A Choice of Kipling's Prose* (London: Faber and Faber, 1987), 334.

page 95. Virginia Woolf, *Women and Writing* (New York: Harcourt, 1980), 116.

page 95. Penelope Vita-Finzi, *Edith Wharton and the Art of Fiction* (New York: St. Martin's, 1990), 21.

page 96. Shannon Hale, "Our Chum Jane," quoted at www.squeetus.com.

page 97. *The Academy* 1 (February 12, 1870): 119.

page 97. J. B. Priestley and O. B. Davis, eds., *Four English Novels* (New York: Harcourt, Brace and Company, 1960), 257.

page 98. E. M. Forster, "Jane Austen," in *Abinger Harvest* (New York: Harcourt, Brace, 1936), 148.

page 99. Joe Wright, quoted at http://www.associated content.com.

page 100. Ian Littlewood, *Jane Austen: Critical Assessments* (London: Routledge, 1999), 471.

page 100. Harold Bloom, *How to Read and Why* (New York: Scribner, 2000), 156.

page 101. G. K. Chesterton, *The Victorian Age in Literature* (New York: Henry Holt, 1913), 109.

page 102. Mary Stolz, *The English Journal* 64:7 (October, 1975): 84–86.

page 102. Ann Tyler, quoted at http://thebookblogger.com.

page 103. Jean Blackall, "Valorizing the Commonplace: Harper Lee's Response to Jane Austen," in Alice Petry, ed., *On Harper Lee: Essays and Reflections* (Knoxville: University of Tennessee Press, 2007.)

page 103. Anthony Lane, "The Dumbing of Emma," *New Yorker*, August 5, 1996, 76.

page 104. Patricia T. O'Conner, "The Jane Austen Book Club: Mr. Darcy Is a Boorish Snob. Please Discuss," *New York Times*, May 2, 2004.

page 104. Michael A. Scully, "Sense as Psychotherapist," *National Review* 18, March 1983, 329.

page 105. Susanna Clarke, quoted at www.bbc.co.uk.

page 108. Mark Twain, *Mark My Words: Mark Twain on Writing*, ed. Mark Dawidziak (New York: St. Martin's, 1996), 128.

page 109. Frederic Harrison, letter to Thomas Hardy, quoted
in Christopher Kent, "Learning History with,
and from, Jane Austen," in J. David Grey, ed., *Jane
Austen's Beginnings: The Juvenilia and Lady Susan*
(Ann Arbor and London: UMI Research Press,
1989), 59.

page 110. D. H. Lawrence, *Apropos of Lady Chatterley's Lover*
(London: Martin Secker, 1931), 93.

page 110. Quoted in Natalie Tyler, ed., *The Friendly Jane Austen*
(New York: Penguin, 1999), 231.

page 111. Ralph Waldo Emerson, *Journals of Ralph Waldo
Emerson* (New York: Houghton Mifflin, 1913), 336.

page 112. T. J. Wise and J. A. Symington, eds., *The Brontës:
Their Friendships, Lives and Correspondence*
(Philadelphia: Porcupine, 1980), 2:180.

page 113. Salmon Rushdie, *The Paris Review*, Issue 174,
Summer 2005.

page 114. Gabriele Annan, "Not So Close to Colette," *The New
York Review of Books*, April 26, 1984, 31:7.

page 115. Julia Braun Kessler, "Murdering Miss Austen,"
California Literary Review, December 6, 2007.

page 116. Rebecca West, *The Strange Necessity* (London:
Jonathan Cape, 1928), 263.

page 117. D. W. Harding, "Regulated Hated: An Aspect of the
Work of Jane Austen," *Scrutiny* 8 (March 1940): 347.